WIN!

How to succeed in the new game of business

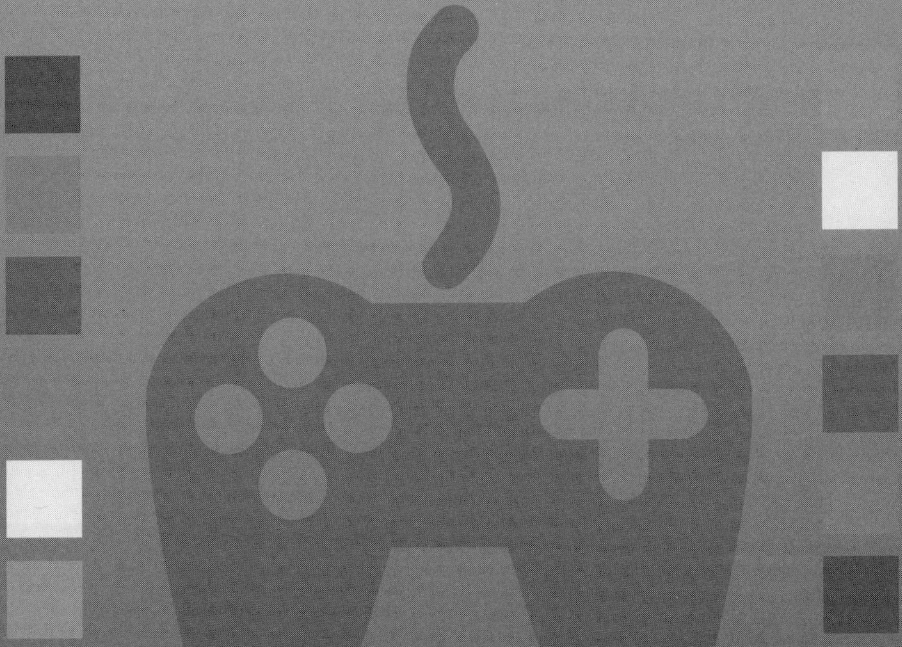

ROGER HARROP

WIN! How to succeed in the new game of business

By Roger Harrop

WIN! How to succeed in the new game of business

paperback ISBN 978-1-909116-38-2
eISBN 978-1-909116-39-9

Published in 2014 by SRA Books
The right of Roger Harrop to be identified as the author of this work has been asserted by him in accordance with the Copyright, Designs and Patents Act 1988.

A CIP record of this book is available from the British Library.

Printed in the UK by TJ International, Padstow, Cornwall.

Thanks to the megastars that are:

Sue Richardson

Neil Brewster

Ayd Instone

Vicky Cheadle

Christine LeHeup

Let's get the ball rolling …

These really are the most exciting of times for business! Nothing is a given any more. Technology is moving at an incredible speed and the winners are keeping it simple – because it is!

Someone wants to buy, someone wants to sell and maybe someone needs to make something. That's it.

Talking of technology, if you want to get the multimedia bonus benefits from this book, you need a smartphone to get access through QR codes to all kinds of additional bonus information I'm giving you and to download and use the interactive app for the book.

What kit you'll need

It may not look like it but you are holding a high-tech book with access to videos, white papers, animations, interactive business health checks and more! Indeed everything to help you win in this new game of business.

So how do you maximise the winning value available in this book?

First, you'll see there are QR codes throughout which gain you access to materials through your tablet or smartphone. To do this you will need to download a free QR reader and I would recommend one of these:

QuickScan

RedLaser

ScanLife

Second, I strongly recommend that you download the free app for the book. Scan the QR code below to be sent to a webpage with instructions on how to download and use the app.

Now you're all set.

You'll find there are a couple of business health checks in the book which, if you choose, you can complete through the app and I recommend you do this regularly. If you do, the app will retain your results and show the trends for your business to make sure you really are winning!

About the author

Roger Harrop BSc(Hons), CEng, FIMechE, FCIM, FInstIB, FPSA, PSAE, CSPGlobal

Roger Harrop has spent over 25 years leading international businesses, including a plc, which puts him in a unique position to deal with present-day business challenges.

Based in Oxford in the UK, he's an international business growth speaker who inspires and entertains audiences with his acclaimed Staying in the Helicopter® programmes. Over 20,000 CEOs, business leaders and others across 38 countries have achieved transformational change through his thought-provoking and entertaining talks laced with real-life stories and humour.

Roger is also an author, business advisor, mentor, consultant and independent director.

He has unusually wide leadership experience ... from small start-ups to multinationals ... and from high-tech products to basic commodities, people-based service businesses and not-for-profit organisations.

Roger spent seven years as Group Chief Executive of a FTSE quoted, high-tech industrial group with 12 sites across 4 continents. The UK Government mentioned it in its 'Competitiveness' White Paper. The US *Forbes* magazine included the group among its list of the top 100 overseas companies. Two business schools have used it as a benchmark case study on culture change and business re-engineering.

Roger has tutored on a leading leadership and teambuilding programme for over 25 years.

He's a keen windsurfer, mountain biker and classic car enthusiast.

Accreditations

Chartered Engineer

Member of the Global Speakers Federation

Fellow of The Chartered Institute of Marketing

Fellow of the Institute for Independent Business

Liveryman with The Worshipful Company of Marketors

Fellow and Past President of the Professional Speaking Association

Former Vice-President and Fellow of the Institution of Mechanical Engineers

Speaker of the Year with The Academy for Chief Executives 2005 and 2011

Ranked in the top 10 of Management and Strategy speakers worldwide

Winner of the Professional Speaking Award of Excellence

Certified Speaking Professional Global

www.rogerharrop.com

Roger's video introduction.

Contents

1 Introduction
The State of Play

Introduction The State of Play

Business is simple. Somebody wants to buy. Somebody has something to sell. Maybe somebody has to make something. That's all business is … simple.

Without growth a business is dead in the water. Business owners have to get up in the helicopter and spend some time looking at the big picture in order to make growth happen.

When I deliver masterclasses to business owners I ask them the question 'What is holding you back? Why is it that you aren't growing as fast as you'd like?' This is what they tell me:

- team's resistance to change
- finding and keeping talent
- it's the credit crunch
- banks won't lend
- can't get investment
- finding the time for business development
- my people aren't selling
- changing markets
- no plan
- risk averse culture
- no new customers

Are these the sort of issues you are facing in your business? What is it that is stopping you growing as fast as you would like?

Not very long ago, I was delivering the masterclass this book is based on to a group of business owners in the UK. During the coffee break, I was approached by one delegate who said to me, 'Roger, you know all those issues we put on the flip chart this morning? I've just realised something … none of them are real are they? I mean, in actual fact, they are just excuses … aren't they? The reason we are not growing as fast as I would like is me – nothing else!'

Top sports people don't make excuses. They play, run or hit to win. Coming second is not an option in their game. Nor should it be in business. In this book I'd like to explore with you what excuses you might be making and what you are allowing to get in the way of your business winning the game and growing to become number one.

What I'm seeing right now in the business world is that the companies that are really flying are those that have gone back to the basics of business. It doesn't matter what sector they're in, it doesn't matter what size they are or where they are in the world, when a company focuses on the four basics of business they really can't fail. So here in this book I will show you how, by focusing on these basics, you too can succeed in what I'm calling 'the new game of business'.

- Win! By being exceptional
- Win! By being a great place to work ... and play
- Win! By constantly prospecting
- Win! By focusing on the score – your bottom line

In today's game of business there is a significant levelling of the playing field going on. I believe these are the most exciting of times for business and there has never been a better time than now – ever – to be in business. Thanks to the shrinking of the world principally through technology, a small company can now run rings around a much bigger business. The sky really is the limit, no matter what size of organisation you are and no matter where you are in the world.

I'm fascinated by giant killers, people who have taken on the biggest in the world and won. In 1987 Red Bull was started by Dieter Mateschitz, an Austrian who had seen tuk-tuk drivers in Bangkok drinking various home-brewed concoctions to keep them going through the day. Unable to raise bank finance for his 'energy drink' (an entirely new concept at the time), he borrowed a few thousand euros from his family and got the company off the ground. Red Bull is sold as a high caffeine drink although in reality the caffeine content of one can of Red Bull is exactly the same as one cup of coffee. Nowadays it is sold in 154 countries and is now the drink of choice of those Bangkok tuk-tuk drivers!

Figure 1 shows the retail prices per gallon of various liquids in the US. Coke is $5.12 a gallon, milk is $11.52 and gasoline is $3.40. Evian water is $8.96 a gallon. Not bad. Budweiser is about $12.63 a gallon.

Red Bull is a remarkable $39.68 a gallon!

Figure 1

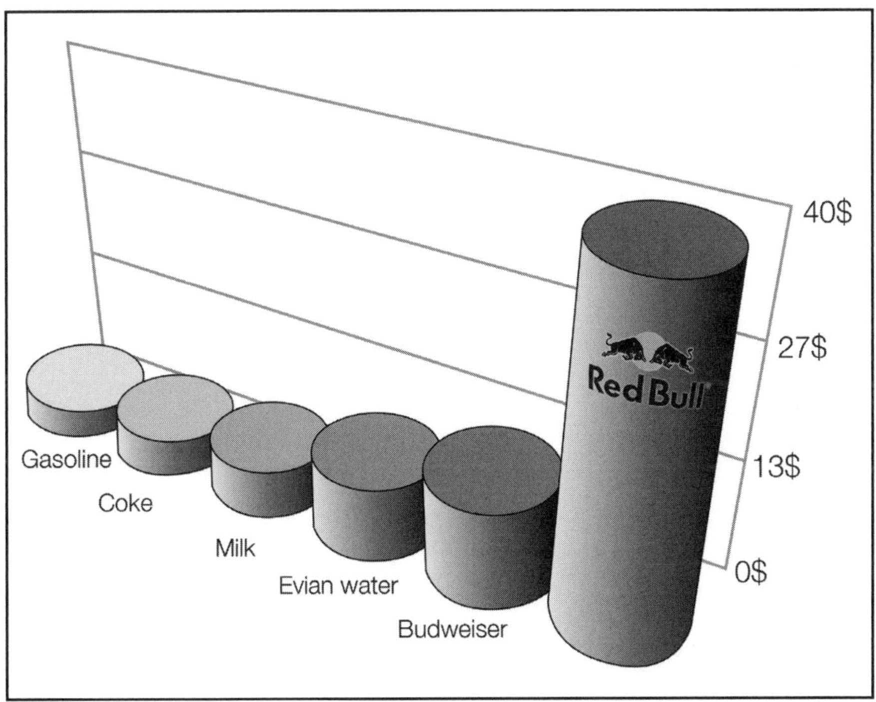

Why do I show you this? In the corporate world people – mostly finance people – are forever talking about 'the average' in their industry. The average margins, the average prices … Do we really win the game by being average or even by being a bit better than average? No, I think not!

So how can we become winners in this new game of business? First and foremost, like Red Bull, we have to be absolutely exceptional.

Chapter One

Win! By Being Exceptional

Chapter One Win! By Being Exceptional

- It's no longer about being good enough at what you do.
- It's no longer good enough to be outstanding at what you do.
- Quite simply you have to be exceptional at what you do; and,
- At *absolutely everything* that you do and *everywhere* that you do it.

Never be afraid of the competition

There is a whole new dynamic at play in the world of business today. The fact is that no one can be mediocre anymore. Frankly, if you, your product or your service are mediocre you're finished. Or you're about to be.

Take a look for a moment at what you do or what you make. If you are really objective about it, what do you see? Is it actually pretty much the same as everyone else's? Maybe it's a little better or a little worse? Essentially, it's probably much the same.

So how can you take the lead in a world where so many are doing or making the same thing? How can you differentiate yourself from the competition?

Let's take another look at Red Bull. They didn't achieve their remarkable success by focusing on the average. They must have roughly the same production costs as Coke and yet the margins they're making are phenomenal. Exceptional companies don't set their aspirations by looking back at the competition, nor accepting industry norms. Just imagine, if before Red Bull launched in the US they had gone to a top consulting firm for advice. What would those consultants have said in return for their big fat fee?

- 'Don't even think about selling it in anything but a standard-sized US can!'

And probably,

- 'Set your prices just below Coke.'

Did they do that? You bet they didn't!

Red Bull shows us we should never be frightened of the competition. Never get into the mindset of 'You know what? We may never be number 1', because if you think like that you will only ever be number 2. You can do anything. It's up to you. There are so many examples these days of organisations that have come from nothing to dominating the world and done it incredibly quickly. We can all do it. It is only us that can limit our potential to grow.

In sport it's recognised that if you're in the lead and you spend too much time looking back at those following you, the gap between you will get smaller. It's the same in business. You certainly need to know your competitors inside out. But you need to run your own race, play your own game and set your own strategy, not theirs, to win!

Increasingly, I am seeing that the way by which exceptional organisations differentiate themselves from the competition is the process they take their customers through and I've shown this in Figure 2.

Figure 2

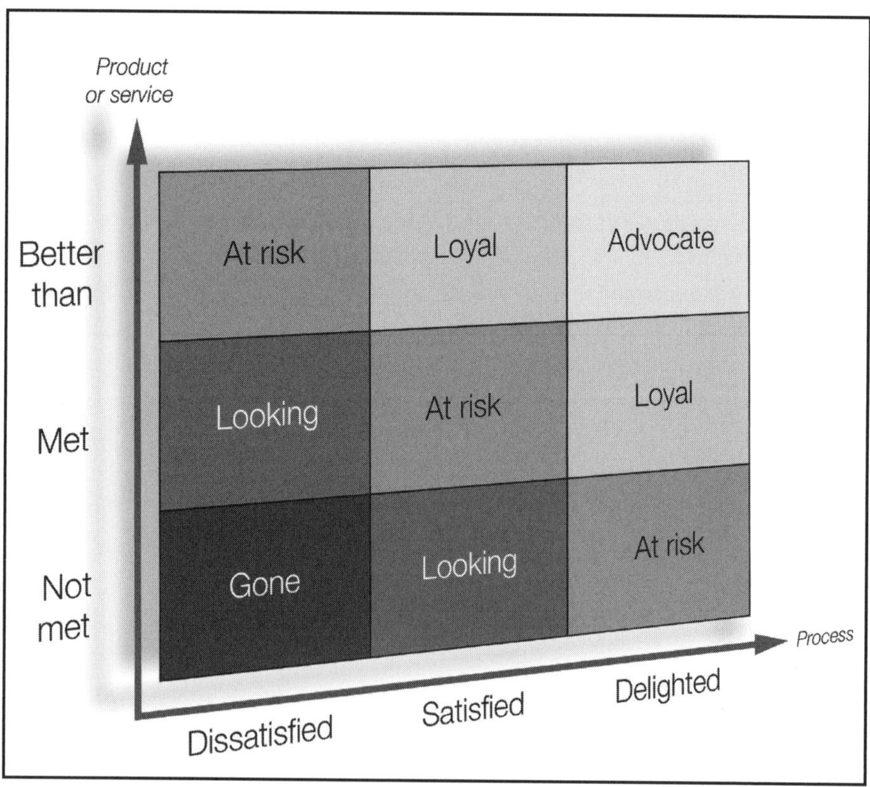

On the Y axis is the status of your product or service in terms of meeting the expectations of your customers: better than expected, met, or not met. On the X axis is the process you take your customers through. Are they dissatisfied, satisfied or delighted?

Let's say you recommend a restaurant to me and I go and have a fantastic meal. It's even better than I expected so my marker will be somewhere on the top line. In reality the food took two hours to come and when it did the waiter had his thumb in the soup. As a dissatisfied customer I end up in the 'at risk' box.

Where you need to have every one of your customers is in the three boxes in the top right corner. These people will be advocates and will be a delight to do business with because they love you. They will be a free sales force because they will tell the world that your company does an outstanding job. The people in the two adjacent boxes will be loyal but anyone else in any other area of this grid you're either at risk of losing or they're already walking away.

When Toyota created Lexus as their luxury car division, their findings from research drove them to the conclusion that as far as the product was concerned, they could not assume they could build a better car than a Mercedes Benz, a BMW or a Jaguar. The only thing they knew was that they could build a car that was as good as one of these market leaders. So they took the strategic corporate decision that they would differentiate themselves in relation to the customer experience.

There is a great story of a man who had been a BMW fan for some years. He put his car in for a service and, as usual, they did a complimentary valet but when it came back the ashtray was missing. He rang up the dealer and said, 'Look I've just got my car back from the service and the ashtray is missing.' The dealer said, 'Don't worry, Mr. Taylor we have it here. Next time you're passing, call in and we'll let you have it.'

He was a bit unhappy with that. So he rang the local Lexus dealer and said, 'Can I ask you a question? If I had a Lexus and I put my car in for a service and it came back and the ashtray was missing, what would you do?' Their reply was instantaneous, 'Why Mr. Taylor we would bring it out to you. Why do you ask?' So he told them.

Two hours later the Lexus dealer delivered his BMW ashtray.

Guess what car he's driving now?

That's the world we are now living in – where 100 per cent is no longer good enough. Every time and everywhere you touch a client or a customer you have to be giving 110 per cent.

Exceptional companies set their own rules. They decide what they are going to achieve, where they are going to go and how they're going to get there.

United Breaks Guitars video

Also these days we are constantly being reminded via social media of what can happen when it all goes wrong and how the ordinary man and woman in the street have a lot of power today. You may have seen the video Dave Carroll and his band put on YouTube about their experience with United Airlines in the US. (Take a look through the QR code on the left). It's now had over 14 million views!

The individual has tremendous power these days – particularly through social media. Another example is a New York guy, a keen cyclist who bought Kryptonite's most expensive $100 bike lock then found, remarkably, that he could open it with a Bic pen! So he wrote to Kryptonite. They ignored him. He wrote again. Then he wrote again and still got nothing – no customer service representative replying, no phone call, no response whatsoever.

Kryponite bike lock video

So he tweeted about it, blogged and posted on all sorts of social media sites and in so doing discovered that, surprise, surprise, hundreds of people who had used the same Kryptonite locks had had their bikes stolen.

This led to a $125 million class action lawsuit, which Kryponite lost, leading to a worldwide total recall of the product.

Do you have a fast response plan in place to respond to an adverse You Tube or other posting about you in social media? You should have.

Who's in your team?

We can't be exceptional unless we have exceptional people and as you will see in Figure 8 later in the book talent is going to be in short supply worldwide through to 2030 at least. You cannot afford to have any passengers. You need to train people, encourage them, nurture them and develop them, but you need people who score 10 out of 10 throughout your organisation.

I understand that Google have a simple philosophy when it comes to recruiting: A-class people recruit A-class people, whereas B-class people tend to only recruit B- and C-class people. So each of Google's top A-class talent is asked to spend time as a recruiter to ensure that they are only ever employing A-class exceptional talent.

As well as employing the best, we of course have to think about how we are going to get the best out of our people. Whenever we talk about people and how they function in an organisation we need to think about teams and we all seek to have genuinely performing teams – those that are many times the sum of the parts. Team performance comes from four things:

1. The people within the teams: their skills and behavioural profiles.
2. The leaders: providing direction, motivation, organisation and structure. (That's your job!)
3. The relationships within the team: mutual trust, respect and support.
4. The atmosphere and the culture in the team.

Over many years Professor Meredith Belbin of Cambridge University together with Henley Business School in the UK looked at teams and the roles within teams that people most prefer to take as well as those they least prefer. They came up with nine roles:

- Shaper: This person is focused on the end objective like a laser beam. Isn't too fussed about how you get there but keeps the team honest. They know where everyone is going and will not waiver. They tend to be objective, challenging, dynamic sorts of people.
- Coordinator/Chair: Clarifies goals, promotes decisions and delegates.
- The Plant: The creative member of the team. I've often had to get hold of chief executives when they're downsizing with a red pen to tell them not to cross out the creative. Business owners think they're a pain to manage because quite often they are. So a CEO thinks, 'What do they do anyway? Let's get rid of them!' I would argue that you need twice as many creatives these days. They're unorthodox but they solve difficult problems.
- Resource investigator: Most salespeople are resource investigators. They explore opportunities external to the team for the benefit of the team.
- Team worker: These are the 'people people' in the team. They are perceptive of how people are feeling. If there's a conflict within the team they are the people most likely to go and try to sort that conflict out for the benefit of the team. They're perceptive, diplomatic and cooperative.

- Implementer: These people are the opposite of team workers. They are 'things people'. They're practical and reliable and turn ideas into action. The Japanese are brilliant implementers. It's what they've built their nation on.
- Monitor evaluator: Most accountants are monitor evaluators. They see the options, they're logical and analytical. Generally shapers and monitor evaluators tend not to get on. Shapers just want to get there while monitor evaluators want to do it in small increments. Usually to three decimal places!
- Completer-finisher: Just that. Painstaking, conscientious, they polish and perfect, not letting the team move on until every 'i' is dotted and every 't' is crossed.
- Specialist: They aren't strictly a member of the team – you bring them in to do a specific job. To be honest, they often can't even spell the word 'people'. They're single-minded, self-starting and dedicated. You bring them in to do the job and then move them out again.

Figure 3

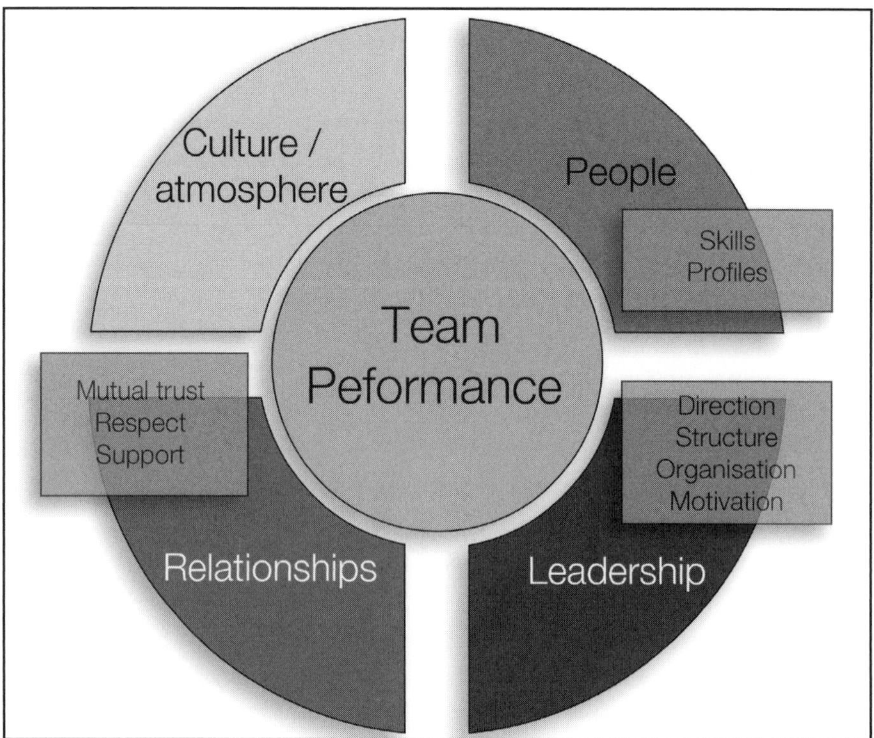

So why are these team roles important? First, if you have a task that needs completing or a project that needs doing each of these roles comes into play at a different stage in the process.

Figure 4

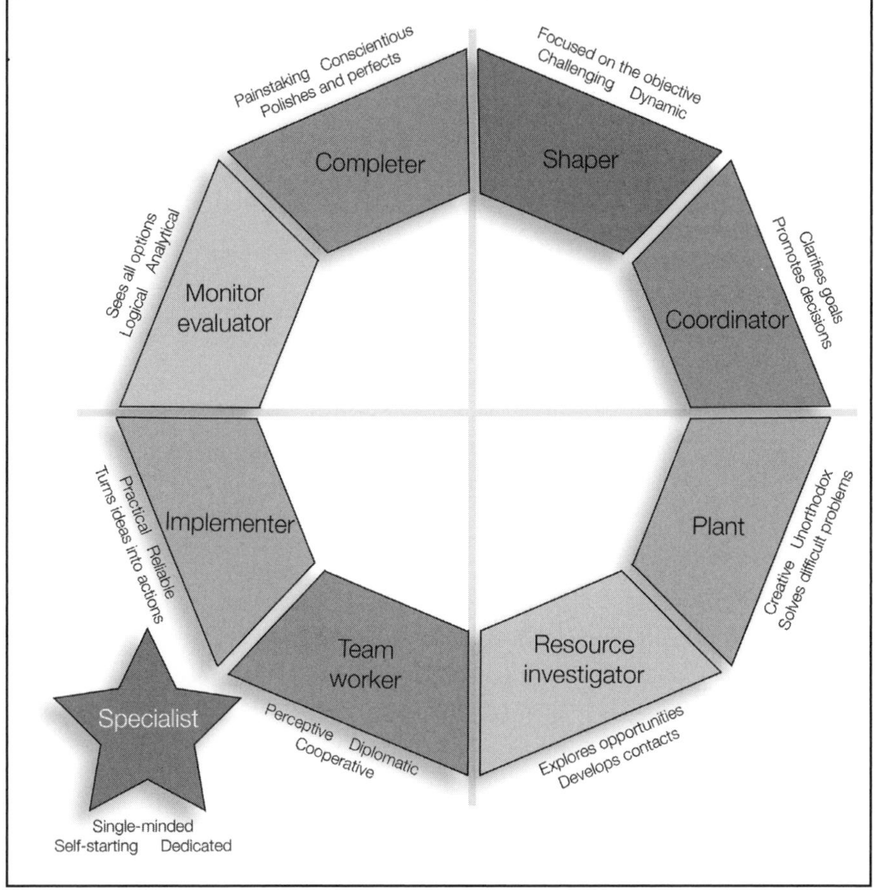

- The first person you need is the shaper to define the objective.
- Then the coordinator starts to marshal resources – both human and physical.
- Next comes the plant, the creative, the ideas person to come up with the options about how you're going to solve the problems.
- Then the resource investigator starts using external contacts for the benefit of the team.

- After that you need the monitor evaluator to do all the checks and balances.
- Finally, the completer-finisher will make sure everything is tied up with a neat ribbon.

If you don't have the people in that order you'll still get the job done. It will just take twice as long.

There's a second powerful reason, however, why these roles are important for organisations who want to be winners.

I was a tutor for over 25 years with Europe's premier experiential leadership programme. I would spend five days with a group of eight or nine individuals who did not know each other and had been randomly selected and they would go through a series of projects – some cerebral, some physical and they would take turns at leading and at following. I can say, just from my observations over 25 years alone, that absolutely no team will work unless it contains at least one person from each of the four quadrants on the illustration. It doesn't matter how skilled and experienced the members are, nor how good the systems and processes, without the four types being represented the team simply will not perform.

I recall in one of the businesses I ran – a high-tech electronics and engineering business – we were using 'simultaneous engineering' to develop new products. This is where you have a multi-disciplined team of people who sit together to develop the products. We had three teams running and none of them were quite getting there. They were getting 80 per cent of the job done and then somehow all the activity dissipated.

Belbin team roles

I got fed up with this so I set up an investigation. We looked at people's CVs and their skill sets, as well as at the procedures we were using and we couldn't find any reason for the problem. And then we looked at Belbin and discovered that, quite by chance, in all three teams we had no one from the top left quadrant. So they really were getting three-quarters of the job done and then they got bored. So all I did was to parachute someone from that quadrant to each team, it didn't matter which discipline they were from. Instantly we started getting new products out on time, every time.

This tool is really powerful and I commend it to you. If you want to have an exceptional business you have to have it full of exceptional teams. There are all kinds of systems you can use. I tend to use Belbin with my clients because it's really down to earth and it isn't designed for HR people. It's designed for those of us who actually run businesses to do so better and more efficiently!

Technology is the game changer

The world has changed – the world of business has changed – and it's all around new technology, which is arriving at eye watering speeds and is set to go exponential!

None of us can afford to ignore it.

The playing field is being levelled – both internationally and between companies – small and large, established and start-up. This really is the most exciting of times to be in business! Internationally, all you need is broadband and a spark in your head and you have the same advantage as anyone else. For example, there is much talk about 'Silicone Safari' at present – which is a group of software engineers in Nairobi that are achieving extraordinary things. During a recent visit to Pakistan I discovered that Lahore is becoming a centre for app development and not just for business applications – remarkably the incidence of Dengue fever in Lahore has been dramatically reduced solely due to a locally developed app.

Pakistan story

Whatever they are selling and wherever they are in the world, I'm seeing small and medium enterprises starting to run rings round many big corporations. They are doing it by swiftly adopting the latest innovations in technology in a way which larger companies often find difficult. What's so new and different, apart from anything else, is that a lot of this technology (and there is so much of it) is free or at least very cheap. It's not just for the techies. This assumption has been mistakenly made – and continues to be so – by many business leaders. It's highly accessible and available to any business who chooses to embrace it.

Another error I see many business leaders making is thinking that this new technology is just for one particular area of the business, such as design or sales and marketing. Varying aspects of technology may find application in any area of the business. It is quite clear that a fundamental core competence of any successful business in the future will be the ability to use new technology as it appears on their radar and to pick it up and run with it quickly – and in absolutely every area of the business.

The technologies that are arriving on the scene now therefore must not be allowed to disappear into one area of the business or another. In order to maximise its effective adoption throughout the company, it is hugely important that the awareness of this constantly emerging groundbreaking new 'stuff' is up at board level. It has to be rooted in the consciousness of the business leader, who is in position to see where in the company any new innovations should be adopted.

If this isn't happening in your company now, then a culture change is required to make sure it happens tomorrow.

The key is to assimilate, adapt and adopt.

- Assimilate the very latest in technology.
- Adapt it to make it work for you in your business.
- Adopt it incredibly quickly. It's probably out of date already!

So how do you discover and assimilate this technology? To put it simply, you need millennials.

Figure 5

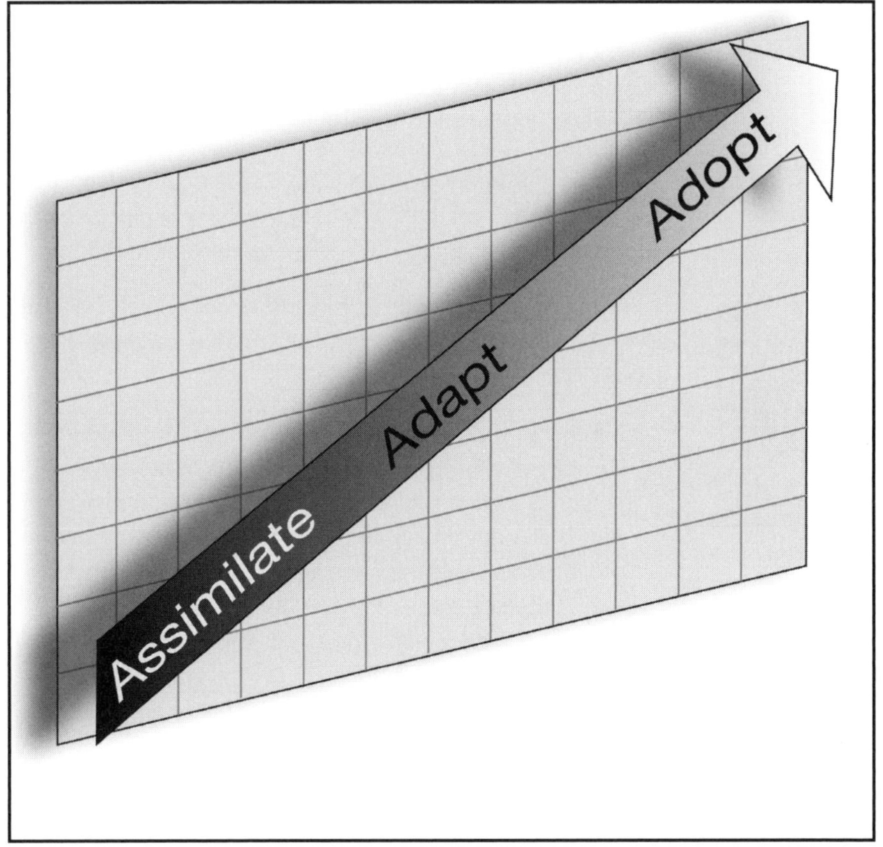

Getting young people onside

I read recently that in the West, 34 per cent of people between the ages of 17 and 30, the so-called millennials, carry out every transaction in their life through their smartphone. So if you can't deal with them in that way they simply won't buy from you. If your website isn't smartphone friendly you're losing customers.

It goes further than that – Professor Sir Steve Smith, Vice Chancellor of Exeter University has said that email is now dead for most students. 'There is no point in emailing students anymore,' he said, 'They get in touch with us by social media, especially Twitter, and we've had to employ people to reply that way.'

Who in your organisation even knows what exists in the way of new technology? For the first time in history, young people have more knowledge than older or more experienced employees.

PwC 'Millennials at Work' white paper

A white paper produced by PricewaterhouseCoopers, 'Millennials at Work: Reshaping the workplace' makes particularly interesting reading.

> Millennials' use of technology clearly sets them apart. One of the defining characteristics of the millennial generation is their affinity with the digital world. They have grown up with broadband, smartphones, laptops and social media being the norm and expect instant access to information. This is the first generation to enter the workplace with a better grasp of a key business tool than more senior workers.

What does this mean to us as business leaders?

Firstly we have got to find a way to bring millennials into our company and have them respected and listened to – and not just in the traditional way of 'start on the bottom rung of the ladder'. Indeed I'm telling larger companies, more than half seriously, that they need to appoint a 'CTEO' – a Chief Technology Exploitation Officer and move them on when they reach the age of 30!

Exceptional companies both now and increasingly in the future will have mechanisms in place to welcome and motivate millennials and effectively utilise them to assimilate and adapt the new technology. These companies will have the 'can do' culture which together with a lack of bureaucracy allows them to be exceptionally fleet of foot.

That means we have to do the same.

That's the world we're in now.

Technology must not be allowed to disappear into a silo

One of the reasons why smaller businesses are often beating larger companies in the new technology space is simply because they don't have departmental silos and they lack big company inertia. They can very quickly assimilate the new stuff, see how it might be used to advantage – anywhere in the business – and then move very quickly to get it done. Most larger companies have silos – operations, sales and marketing, finance – and new technology can get lost in any one of them.

Take 3D printing. Now, 3D printing is not new. In fact it's been around for 25 years. And yet it's only recently that people have started to talk about it as potentially having the same impact on the world as the Industrial Revolution.

Twenty five years ago, 3D printing was called 'rapid prototyping' by the engineers and it stayed with them for the next 20-odd years. It's only now that 3D printing has started to be used to advantage in other areas. There are amazing technical things that can be done with 3D printing of course, such as titanium parts for satellites and aircraft. Almost 20 per cent of replacement knee joints are now being 3D printed. And because there are no set-up costs, and it costs the same to print one item as it does to print 10,000, this means your new knee could be made to be unique to you – mimicking your own joint when it was healthy.

What we are now seeing, however, is the creative use of 3D printing in all kinds of applications and areas of the organisation. I understand that McDonald's are actively considering putting one in each of their restaurants. The printers would create McDonald's Happy Meal dolls – perhaps even reproduced with the individual child customer's face. What would that do for revenues?

It's not just polymers and metals either. There's a start-up company in Spain that's printing chocolate! On Valentine's Day you can send a chocolate with your own portrait printed on it for your loved one. In fact there is lots of research and development going on into 3D printing many kinds of food.

One Belgian insurance company is using 3D printing as a value-added service for their customers. All policy-holders are invited to have their front door keys scanned by the company so that in the event of them losing their keys they can be either sent the scan to take to their local 3D printing shop, or be sent a set of replacement keys within a few hours. This is proving highly effective in increasing the company's sales of home insurance policies.

Recently, the Japanese retailer Muji together with the airline ANA created a competition using 3D printers in each of their stores. To enter the competition, a customer would have themselves scanned in store and the winner flown by ANA to some exotic location where they would be reunited with themselves! Mini scale models of customers were created from the scans using 3D printers in a clever marketing campaign that netted Muji a significant increase in footfall in their shops.

3D printing video

If you are not wholly sure what 3D printing is about have a look at the video through the QR.

Innovation can come cheap – or even free!

The cost of 3D printers may be coming down rapidly – in fact, you can now purchase your own online for under £2,000. Yet there are technologies that are completely free. QR codes, for example, are becoming ubiquitous. In fact, if you're not using them you're likely to be losing sales and losing advantage.

One client of mine didn't send Christmas cards last year – they sent QR codes with a personalised video from the CEO for each client in their own language. At the very least that's going to get people talking about them. Because it's new and different – and it costs nothing!

Have a look at this JCPenney ad through the QR.

JCPenney video

Like 3D printers, though, QR codes aren't just for one area of the organisation like sales and marketing. They can also have an important impact on productivity for example, for those who are using them cleverly. In Wales QR codes appear on all doctors' prescriptions and within the code is embedded whatever the prescription is for. Paul Mayberry owns seven pharmacies in South Wales. Paul has bought himself a robot dispenser. All the prescriptions that come into his seven pharmacies are sent straight to the robot dispenser which works 24/7. It dispenses the drugs and sends them back to the shops. After six months he tells me he has halved his stock and is saving £200,000 a year! That's all about operational efficiency.

Have you considered that sort of an application in your business?

Last year I got a new knee in hospital and the identity bracelet didn't have my name on it, it had a QR code and in there were my entire medical records. Every time any procedure was done to me they came along and scanned it. In a hospital this is surely time saving, money saving – perhaps even potentially life saving.

As well as QR codes, apps are also becoming crucial for businesses. The moment I have your app on my smartphone your company is embedded with me. You will become my first choice of supplier – so why would you not have one? You will already have seen the app that I've had developed to go with this book. It's enabling me (I hope!) to give you considerably enhanced value and make a connection with you through various media.

Augment video

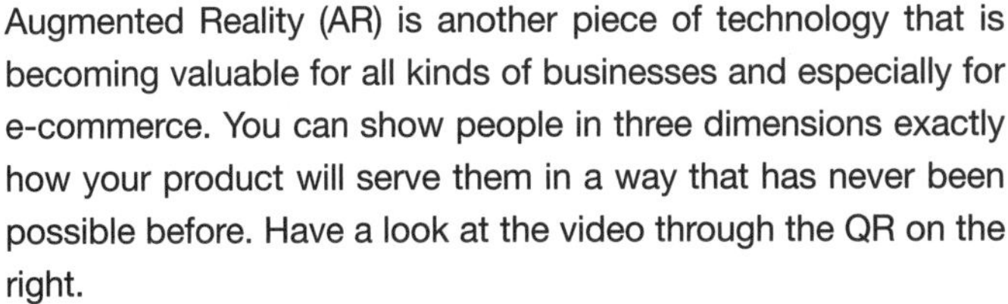

Augmented Reality (AR) is another piece of technology that is becoming valuable for all kinds of businesses and especially for e-commerce. You can show people in three dimensions exactly how your product will serve them in a way that has never been possible before. Have a look at the video through the QR on the right.

Try AR in action!

Download this app and see AR in action on a £10 or €20 note or a dollar bill!

Playing the game of business

'Gamification' is another way businesses are using technology to gain advantage.

Computer video games are incredibly popular worldwide. It is a $100 billion business – and not just for young people but for all ages. Research shows the average gamer today is 35 years old and married and games for 12 hours a week. Playing computer games has now become a major way for people to relax. They have become more interesting, exciting and engaging as the technology has developed.

So how can this now increasingly ubiquitous form of entertainment be used by businesses?

One example of this is the Silver Grill Cafe in Fort Collins, Colorado in the US which was looking for more sales and more employee engagement. They identified that orange juice and cinnamon rolls were high margin products but staff incentive programmes tried previously had failed to help sell more of them.

Online gaming tokens were given to staff in return for sales of these products. Staff members then played point-yielding games that could be converted to dollars. The results were incredible. They achieved employee engagement of 90 per cent and a 24 per cent increase in sales. There was also unexpected benefits: a massive reduction in staff churn and absenteeism.

On the lead generation side, a highly successful 'Surprising Drives' competition put together by Mazda involved customers playing a computer game just to get a test drive of one of their cars! One would think that all one had to do was pick up the phone and ask for a test drive, but this just goes to show how much people enjoy these sorts of engaging tactics and how you can use them to attract them to things you might be giving away anyway!

My final words on technology

To sum up, it's clear that technology is not just for the technical side of any business. We have seen examples of its use in lead generation, customer engagement, sales, operational efficiency, new product development, employee engagement and brand building. There is no area of the business that cannot benefit and there is no area of the business that will not suffer if it isn't using it.

No matter what your business, no matter what size or what sector you are in, no matter what industry, there are new technologies arriving in droves every day that could help you create success in multiple areas of your business – to differentiate you from the competition, grow sales, improve operational efficiency, engage employees or to incorporate in new products. It may not even cost a lot – it is just a question of you as business leader being open to it, knowing about it and adopting it quickly throughout every area of your business.

One note of caution. Whatever technology is new, no matter how up to speed you are, it is probably ancient by the time you become aware of it. Already, for example, there is now 4D printing where the component makes itself! You cannot afford to dawdle so my advice to you is to get those millennials in to help you now!

Remember – new technology is arriving this very minute and the quicker you get to it the more you will be ahead of, or at the very least keep up with, what your competitors are doing.

Technology has helped level the playing field – so get scoring now!

27

Chapter Two

Win! By Being a Great Place to Work ... and Play

Chapter Two Win! By Being a Great Place to Work ... and Play

The war on talent

According to Roland Berger, the German strategy consultants and an expert in long-term trend spotting, we are facing a war on talent in the coming years:

> The United States will need to add 26 million workers to its talent pool by 2030 to sustain the average economic growth of the last twenty years, while Western Europe will need 46 million additional employees. Germany alone will lack 4.4 million people, with about half of that (2.4 million people) required in the academic field, especially in research, consulting, health and education.
>
> (Roland Berger Strategy Consultants)

Our weapons in this war on talent are our abilities to interest, engage, attract and retain the exceptional people we need. It is no longer just a question of you assessing potential employees. They will be assessing you probably even more than you them and you're not going to recruit and retain the best people unless they believe you are giving them a great place to work. Employers want people with a sparkle in their eye and a fire in their belly, but equally those people want to work for employers who are not only going to value them, but whose values they share.

Share your values

The best talent has a choice these days and will simply not work for an organisation whose values they don't share – they would rather not work at all. Your company has to be a great place to work. But it goes much further than that. When you're interviewing someone these days, it is highly likely that they're going to ask *you* what the values of *your* organisation are. (Are they on your website?) If you can't answer that then they'll go and work somewhere else. If you *can* answer the question they'll then ask you to show them how you are living by those values and if you can't answer that they won't work for you.

I'm not a fan of the mission statement. It's usually been designed by a committee and stuck up in reception or on a website to be ignored and if you can't quote it word for word when asked then frankly it has to go.

What you do need, embedded in everyone in the company's hearts and minds are the values of your company. Everyone in the company needs to be clear as to how you live by them and be constantly seeking to do better.

A study by MORI showed that 88 per cent of employees said they wanted to work for an employer who was committed to living its values. Worryingly, only 45 per cent currently believe their employer was actually doing so.

That's not good enough! If you want to have the best people both now and in the future you have to do something about this.

What do employees really want?

Harvard Business Review

A *Harvard Business Review* study asked employees what they wanted from their employer. While this might seem an obvious thing to do, it is astonishing how rarely this sort of research has been done in the past.

The top conclusions of the respondents were:

- I want to know what my role is. I want to know the box I have to work in. I want to know what success looks like.
- I want to see discipline. I want to see my co-workers disciplined if they step out of line. I do not want soft management because it's unfair.
- I want to be excited when I come to work. I spend more time awake at work than I do at home so I want to get up every morning and look forward to coming to work no matter what my job is.
- I want praise.

When I had just graduated my first boss was an exceptional man called Arthur Shillito and I have tried to emulate him throughout my career. If I had a meeting with Arthur and a third party – a customer or supplier say – often within an hour of the meeting a handwritten note would appear on my desk:

Roger, thank you so much for your contribution to the meeting, I really appreciate it. Arthur.

I was a young guy and every time I got one of Arthur's notes my shoulders would go back, and my chest would go out. There was nothing I wouldn't do for Arthur. It was the praise that made me feel that way. It wasn't about the money. It's worth noting, by the way, that in this list of what employees want money isn't mentioned.

However much praise you've been giving, please give two or three times more. I'm not talking just about the people down the line from you but about your peer group as well. There's absolutely nothing wrong with saying, 'That's a brilliant idea! Well done!' And why not praise your boss? 'That was a good initiative you came up with there.' We all need praise. It's a basic human need.

- Don't scare me.

This worried me when I first saw it. As a boss I always believed we needed that Dunkirk spirit of, 'We're all in this together and we can face whatever is thrown at us'. Then I realised that what this really means is not, 'Please don't tell us what is going on when times are tough,' but rather, 'Please don't scare us for the sake of it'. 'Please tell us when you are clear exactly what you want us to do, not before.'

- I want to be impressed by my boss.
- Give me autonomy.

What they are saying here is, 'It doesn't matter how young I am or how inexperienced, please trust me. Do not micro-manage me.' Don't abrogate your management responsibility – still do all the usual checks and balances, but give more autonomy and responsibility.

- I want to be part of a winning organisation. I want to be able to go home at night and say, 'Yes! We're getting there!'

Figure 6

What Employees Want

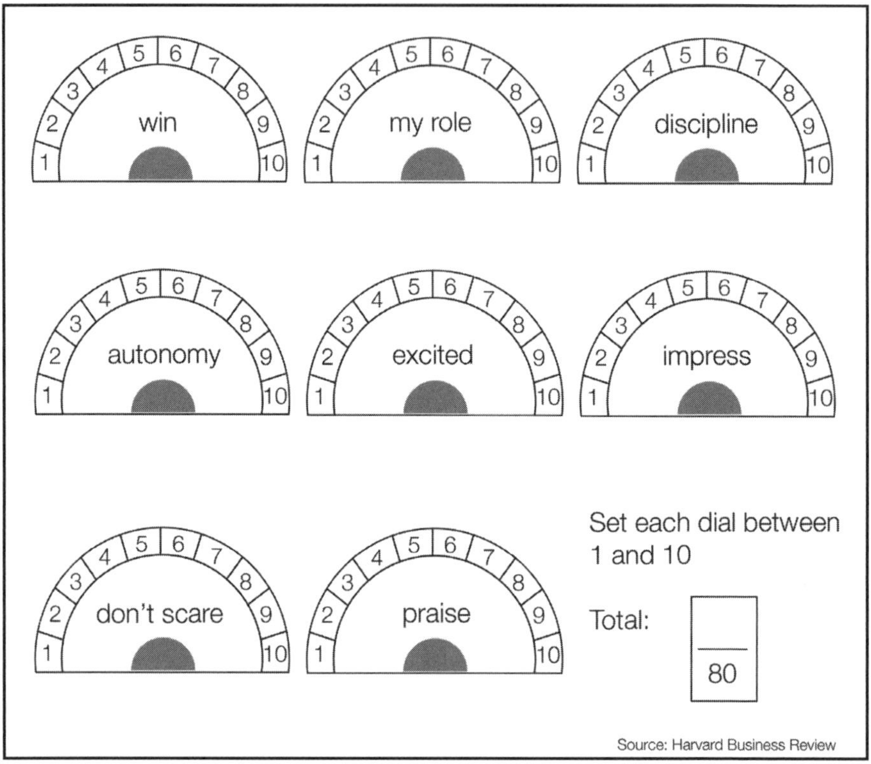

win — 1 2 3 4 5 6 7 8 9 10

my role — 1 2 3 4 5 6 7 8 9 10

discipline — 1 2 3 4 5 6 7 8 9 10

autonomy — 1 2 3 4 5 6 7 8 9 10

excited — 1 2 3 4 5 6 7 8 9 10

impress — 1 2 3 4 5 6 7 8 9 10

don't scare — 1 2 3 4 5 6 7 8 9 10

praise — 1 2 3 4 5 6 7 8 9 10

Set each dial between 1 and 10

Total: ___ / 80

Source: Harvard Business Review

So, if I was to come in and do a confidential survey of your employees, what would the average score for your company be out of 80 on Figure 6?

Select the What Employees Want icon on the app Home screen

You can complete this health check through the app. Score your view for each of the eight areas of what you think your employees might give.

What score is acceptable? What score indicates that you have a culture of motivating and retaining the talent you have?

Like every area of business it's always the dynamic that's important. Whatever you score now, it's important that when you check it again in three or six months that you have moved forward a notch or two. However, if your score is lower than 70 I would suggest that you are not in the first division of exceptional organisations and you need to do better.

Money is not the driver

As we have seen, money does not feature in the top 10 list above of things employees really want. That is because, in reality, money is not the primary driver.

I was recently asked by the owner of a recruitment company about one of her consultants. He was a young man who she was finding really difficult to motivate. She told me that he was still living at home, she was paying him a good salary and his parents were giving him £10 a week pocket money – at 27! She wanted to know what she could do about the situation.

That young man probably just needed some of the above. As long as we believe money is everything we will continue to miss what it is that employees really want.

There's every reason for work to be fun too. Cosatto Limited have the great strapline 'baby stuff with personality' and work very hard at employee engagement. Whilst visiting them a while back Andrew Kluge, the CEO, told me they were putting in a slide from the first floor down to the ground so I asked him to explain what it was all about:

Cosatto

> The slide was part of a bigger project to create a work, relax and play hub in the physical centre of the business. We wanted to create somewhere that everyone in the company would come to chat, relax, meet, eat and generally be together. The slide has had an enormous effect in many respects. It has generated massive pride within the business as a whole. However bad your day is, however stressed you are – a trip down the slide just demands a smile.

Recruiting, motivating and retaining

I don't think any of us in business these days spend enough time on recruiting and retaining talent. To win in the game of business we have to get really good at putting round pegs in round holes.

I am a believer in using every possible tool to do that and I am an advocate for the use of one-day assessment centres to really evaluate talent. These may appear time consuming and costly, but it's much less expensive to use them than to recruit and train and have to part company with an employee who was never going to be right for the job. The cost of getting it wrong has been estimated as something like four or even five times the employee's annual salary.

Seven Ways Not to Hire Turkeys

There is more about how to recruit and retain good people in my free white paper, *Seven Ways Not to Hire Turkeys*.

It's now more important than ever if there is to be a war on talent through to 2030.

35 Chapter Three

Win! By Constantly Prospecting

Chapter Three Win! By Constantly Prospecting

What do I mean by prospecting?

My definition of prospecting is talking to people who have never bought from you or who have not bought from you in, say, the past three years.

We can simply never take the risk of expecting customers to find us. This strategy that may have worked for some in the past, but now, frankly, it's just too dangerous – you are not in control of your business.

Whomever is responsible for selling in your organisation should be spending at least 20 per cent of their time prospecting. In other words, they should be spending one day a week looking for new leads and talking to them. I could quite happily argue that if you want to grow or you are in a more testing climate your salespeople should be spending an even bigger proportion of their time than that.

This means that if you're a sole trader, for example, you must never fill your diary up with work because if you do, you won't be prospecting and you won't have any future business. This doesn't just apply to small businesses – the same applies to all of us.

It really is a numbers game

There is a relationship between the number of properly pre-qualified leads you have in your business and the business you get. Most companies will measure that at between 5 and 20 per cent. So, between 5 and 20 per cent of the leads you qualify will turn into business.

What this means is that (assuming you have less than 80 per cent market share and therefore have headroom to grow) if you double the number of leads then you will double sales. For my business, I have developed an algebraic formula based on the statistics I collect – inputs and outputs, etc. – and it really works. I know exactly what returns I get from any prospecting I do.

This can work for any kind of business. Okay, I'm an engineer by background and it may not suit everyone – not all business owners will take easily to such a left-brain approach. At the same time, I think we need to get away from the traditional 'seat of the pants' salesman way of doing things. If your sales team is adopting an attitude of wholly right brain, 'Let's get out there and see what we can get,' they won't be as effective.

So, if you generate twice as many leads you will get twice as much business. It really is as simple as that!

What happens if you don't play the prospecting game?

Professional firms – lawyers, accountants, architects and the like – are traditionally the worst culprits. The other day I was speaking to a managing partner of a law firm who simply didn't understand what I was talking about when I mentioned prospecting. He seemed to find the whole idea of 'knocking on doors' beneath them. My hunch is that he and his firm will soon not be in business at all!

A friend of mine is a civil engineer – an expert in the design of ports. He's worked for a big firm of consultants in the UK for many years and is now in his early 60s. For a long time he's been saying he wants to start to pass on his knowledge to the next generation, but to no effect. Then he was approached by a major Australian firm of consultants who had a large programme of building ports to meet the demands of the China-generated boom in Western Australia. They made him an offer he couldn't refuse, to move out there, saying also they wanted to put two young guys alongside him to learn all he knew. The position would be his swan song to what had been a rewarding career.

Not so long ago he was back visiting the UK and he told me something very interesting. He remarked that he had been recruited on the back of the boom and that that boom was now over. China had slowed down and there were now very few new ports under review in Australia. Imagine his surprise when he then discovered that there was no pipeline of other prospects. His large engineering consultancy that had been stacked out with work previously had stopped prospecting. They had allowed themselves to fill every minute of every day with work. Given that it takes at least 12 months for that kind of large-scale engineering project to move through the sales pipeline, the company now has a significant self-imposed challenge ahead just to survive.

Playing the prospecting game and winning

Here is a model that I use when I work with sales forces. The Y axis indicates whether the salesperson is prospecting or not, while the X axis giveS you the measure of effectiveness of your sales force: orders ahead of budget, orders behind budget. It's all pretty basic stuff.

Figure 7

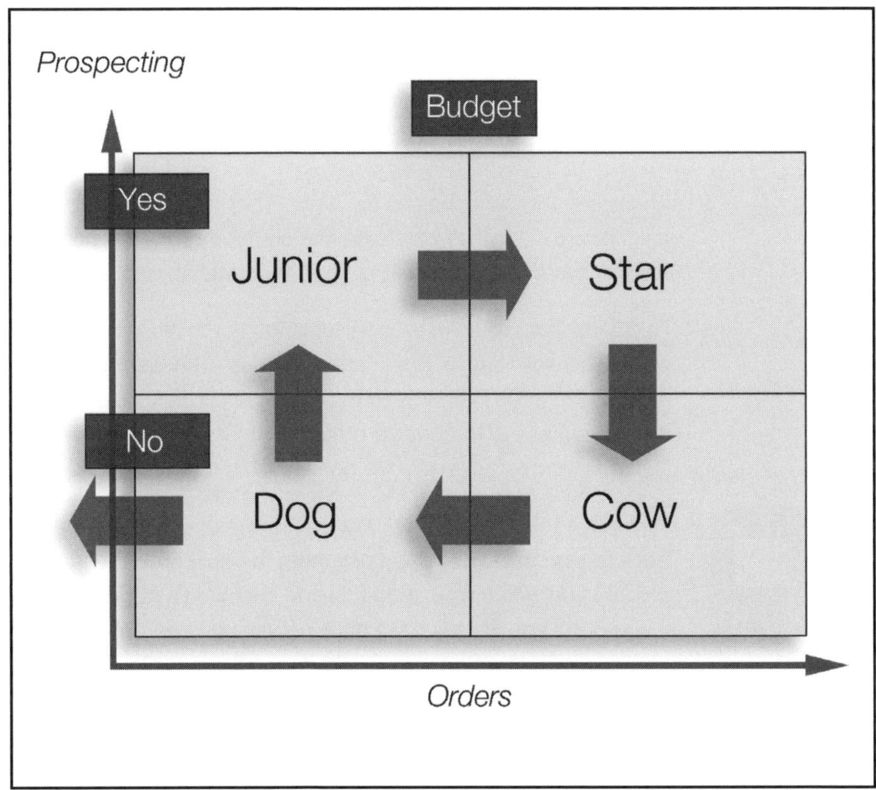

A new salesperson always starts out as a junior. By definition, they are behind budget and everything they do is prospecting. Where you want them to go – indeed where you want to have most of your salespeople – is into the star box. Stars are ahead of budget and they are still prospecting.

So that's where you want the majority of your sales force. It doesn't always work quite like that though, does it? Your sales team members begin to say, 'I have too many demands placed on me by customers and I don't really have the time to prospect anymore. I'm too important to prospect. I'm too busy to prospect,' and they become cash cows.

Without exception, in every sales force I have ever worked with the people who are the most revered aren't the stars, they're the cows. They're ahead of budget but they have stopped prospecting for whatever reason.

The cow box is in fact a pretty dangerous place to be. Suddenly your second biggest customer moves to China, the third biggest one goes under and guess what – the revered cow salesperson is behind budget and has no prospects.

There are only two choices for dogs. They can learn how to be a junior again, or they can leave the company. There is nowhere else for them to go and you have to be brutal about this.

Rarely do I find sales managers looking at or thinking about their people in this way or their effectiveness. The salespeople in each of the three boxes need managing in a totally different way if the business is to achieve a majority of stars. That's the vital job of sales management. No one else can do it.

Select the Sales Management Matrix icon on the app Home screen

Where on this model is your company's sales team? Take this back to your sales force and ask them the question. The app will provide you with a way to do this and check on it regularly. Even if you don't specifically have salespeople you need to ask yourself, 'Where's the centre of gravity of my business?'

Prospecting is a responsibility

Last year I was with a firm of accountants with 21 partners that I've worked with before. The managing partner rang me up in January and asked me if I'd do a masterclass for the first day of their partners' conference that Spring, to which I said fine. It got to two or three weeks before the event and he rang me up again and told me they were going to have to postpone it and asked me if it would be okay if it was held on a Sunday. When I asked him why he told me he'd just made 10 per cent of the staff redundant and he really didn't want them knowing that the conference was being held in a posh hotel.

So, perhaps a little mischievously, I said to him, 'With 10 per cent redundancies, presumably that means there's only going to be 19 partners from now on?' 'Oh no,' he said, 'it doesn't work like that – the partners aren't affected.' At this point I decided I was really going to go for these guys when my day with them came round. I hadn't been planning to show them the sales management matrix model but I was getting so frustrated with what they were saying to me.

I put up the slide and asked them to tell me where the centre of gravity of the partnership was. And guess what? Twenty-one partners, who owned the business, said that they were cow moving to dog. I said, 'So what are you going to do about it?' They all shrugged their shoulders and said, 'Probably nothing.'

I really thought I'd trained myself not to get emotionally involved with my clients, but that night I drove home with white knuckles on my steering wheel. I couldn't help thinking, 'There's going to be a lot more people losing their jobs because of their incompetent management.'

It's irresponsible! A level of arrogance that says, 'Clients will find us.'

I don't care what type or size of organisation you are – commercial, partnership, not-for-profit, member association – you have to prospect if you want to have even a chance of winning.

Checking out the prospects

It always staggers me how many salespeople there are out there who don't use the easily-accessible tool that is social media before they go out and meet a prospect. You can turn a cold lead into a warm lead just by finding out which football team they support, for example.

But it applies to all of us – before you talk to someone you've never met before, adopt the discipline of checking them out on LinkedIn or other social network.

Choosing who to sell to

A basic law of the game of business is to sell to people who've got money!

It may seem obvious but you'd be surprised how many people I've met over the past few years who have been through the recession banging their heads against a brick wall trying to sell to people who can't afford their products or services.

I was in Northampton, UK recently and I met a guy who had a building company. I asked him how business was and he said, 'Fabulous!' When I questioned him he told me that in 2008 when the recession hit them they had nothing. All their business disappeared. He told me that he and his partner got into their helicopter and had a good look. 'We asked each other the question, "Who's got money?".' Now the only building work they do is extensions to London houses that are worth more than £5 million. He said, 'Of course, I have to wear a tie now. And we have a glossy brochure. But we're making more money than you can imagine, with margins that are nothing short of phenomenal.'

There is a golden rule of business: sell to people who have money. It applies to every single one of us.

Global trends

As well as selling to people who have money, you will be riding the crest of a wave if you also sell to people in growing markets. Figure 8 shows key trends I've highlighted from research by consultants Roland Berger, predicting global trends through to 2030.

You will see that between now and 2030 the world population is going to age by five years. That's massive! If you're not in healthcare, get into healthcare! If you're not in nursing homes, get into nursing homes! If you're not in pharmaceuticals, get into pharmaceuticals! If you are operating in these areas you are going to be riding the crest of a wave.

Water demand is going to be up by 53 per cent. If that's a market for you, get in there!

Technology, as we explored in Chapter One, will be moving at even more eye-watering speeds by 2030 and be disseminated around the world extremely quickly. We need to be on top of this if we aim to win in this new game of business.

Figure 8

2030 Global Trends

Demographics	Population	6.9bn to 8.3bn
	Aging	+5 years
	Urbanisation	59%
Globalisation	BRICs GDP	+7.9%pa
	Next 11 GDP	+5.9%pa
Resources	Energy demand	+26%
	Water demand	+53%
	Commodities	Rare metals / food
Climate change	CO_2	+16%
	Warming	+0.5°C to 1.5°C
	Ecosystem	Extremes
Technology	Diffusion	High speed
	Innovation	Change lives
	Life sciences	NBT
Knowledge	Know how	55% in 2ndry edu
	Gender gap	Narrowing
	War for talent	Demand > supply
Responsibility	Cooperation	Nations
	NGOs	+++
	Philanthropy	+++

Source: Roland Berger Strategy Consultants

NGOs (non government organisations) are going to proliferate. If that could be a market you could get into, get into it!

The BRIC economies will be the top economies in the world by 2030. Not America, not Europe, but Brazil, Russia, India and China and on average they're going to grow at 7.9 per cent each year between now and then. I'm selling to, or have plans to sell to, all four of them. Are you? If not, why not?

Then there are the so-called 'Next 11' which are Bangladesh, Egypt, Indonesia, Iran, Mexico, Nigeria, Pakistan, the Philippines, South Korea, Turkey and Vietnam. With average growth rates through to 2030 of 5.9 per cent each year you cannot afford to ignore them. So far I have developed my business in 5 of the 11. Where are you up to?

Finally, I'm always brought up short when I see the illustration below.

Figure 9

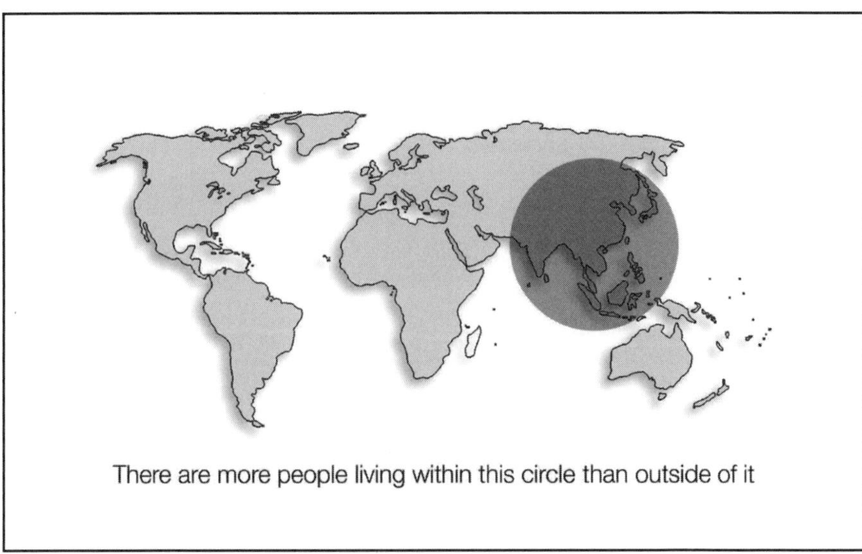

There are more people living within this circle than outside of it

Have you made an objective decision about which pitch in the world is best for you to play your game of business on?

45 Chapter Four

Win! By Focusing on the Score – Your Bottom Line

Chapter Four Win! By Focusing on the Score – Your Bottom Line

Remembering the purpose of being in business

Now we come to what is probably the most obvious of all basics of business. There is nothing new about this and yet it really pays to remind ourselves of what it has to be all about in the first place – the bottom line.

Whilst we will certainly have many objectives for our business, be it in the marketplace, amongst its peers, in the community, country or the environment, we can do none of these things sustainably unless we generate a profit, which we reinvest in part or in whole into the business.

When I work with companies to help them to focus on their sustainable growth, I often start off by asking them about their purpose – why they exist and what success means to them. (See my book *Staying in the Helicopter®: The Key to Profitable Growth*.)

Book
Staying in the Helicopter®

Recently I was working with a firm of architects. There were six shareholders, four of whom were on the board and two of whom were managers. I had the top team of 14 directors and managers in the room.

So I asked my usual question, 'What's the purpose of the business? What is it there for?' I stood at the flip chart and wrote down whatever they said. I got all kinds of answers like, 'We want to be the best architects in the world,' 'We want to save the planet,' and so it went on. And on and on and on …

Well, I was getting to the end of the second page of my flip chart and then, finally, there was this small voice. It was the lady who did the inside administration and she said, 'I'm a shareholder in this business and I'd quite like a return that's better than putting my money in a building society.' There was total silence in the room and then the CEO said, unbelievably, 'We've never thought about that before!'

We spent the whole of the rest of the day and a half's training session talking about what being in business was really all about.

The CEO rang me later and told me what a huge turning point that moment had been for the business. Well, surprise, surprise!

I find it's very easy these days to lose sight of the need for profitability if we wish to grow, especially in the West.

I work a good deal with charities and other 'not-for-profit' organisations and it's easier for them than most to lose sight of the bottom line. Not-for-profit is, in fact, a total misnomer. The term should really be not-for-profit-*distribution*. Most need to generate profits to reinvest in the organisation in order to grow it.

We *all* need to focus on bottom line growth.

A simple measure of growth

When I first started out life in manufacturing there existed this great long formula to measure something called productivity. It involved various people like rate fixers, time and motion clerks and all sorts of considerations that barely exist now. In fact it's all rather fallen into disrepute today and I really don't think it should have done. We don't tend to talk productivity these days, but we ought to. There is one KPI (key performance indicator) that we should all be using and for me it's really simple.

$$\frac{\textbf{sales}}{\textbf{number of people}} = \textbf{£s/\$s/€s}$$

If you set a target to improve that by 10 per cent every single year you will never look back. You will fly. For some businesses this may appear to be too simple in which case the formula could be based on margins or it could be profit rather than sales. If you have a big range of salaries you might use sales/unit cost of payroll. The important thing is that you stick with the same formula – that it's simple and everyone in your business understands it. It is the trend that you are looking at and as long as it is moving forward by at least 10 per cent per annum you will never look back.

This should be a prime KPI for your business that appears on your monthly report.

Getting to new levels of sales

How would you like to double your sales? As we explored in Chapter Three, there is a direct relationship between the amount of time your salespeople spend professionally prospecting and the business you get. If you can double the time they spend sitting in front of pre-qualified leads you will double your business. It really is that easy!

Figure 10 shows some research carried out by Ericsson a few years ago into how a typical field salesperson spends their time. They spend 10 per cent of their time prospecting, which we've already mentioned isn't enough, but it's typical. They spend 23 per cent of their time actively selling. They spend 15 per cent of their time servicing the customer. Then there's a massive 52 per cent of their time that they typically spend on travel and administration.

What that means is they're only spending a third of their time doing what you pay them to do. Is this what it ought to be? We've already said they should be spending at least 20 per cent of their time prospecting. Let's say 25 per cent. Let's change the time they spend actively selling to 35 per cent, leave 15 per cent of their time for service because you can't really get away from that and then it should be no more than 25 per cent on travel and admin. If you can achieve that you will simply double the time they spend sitting in front of properly pre-qualified leads and the consequence of that can only be that you double sales.

Unfortunately, I have rarely come across sales management who thinks like this.

So how do we actually achieve this?

Now I know that many of us don't have sales teams as such these days, or if we do they don't visit customers, but many do and the philosophy still applies to all.

Figure 10

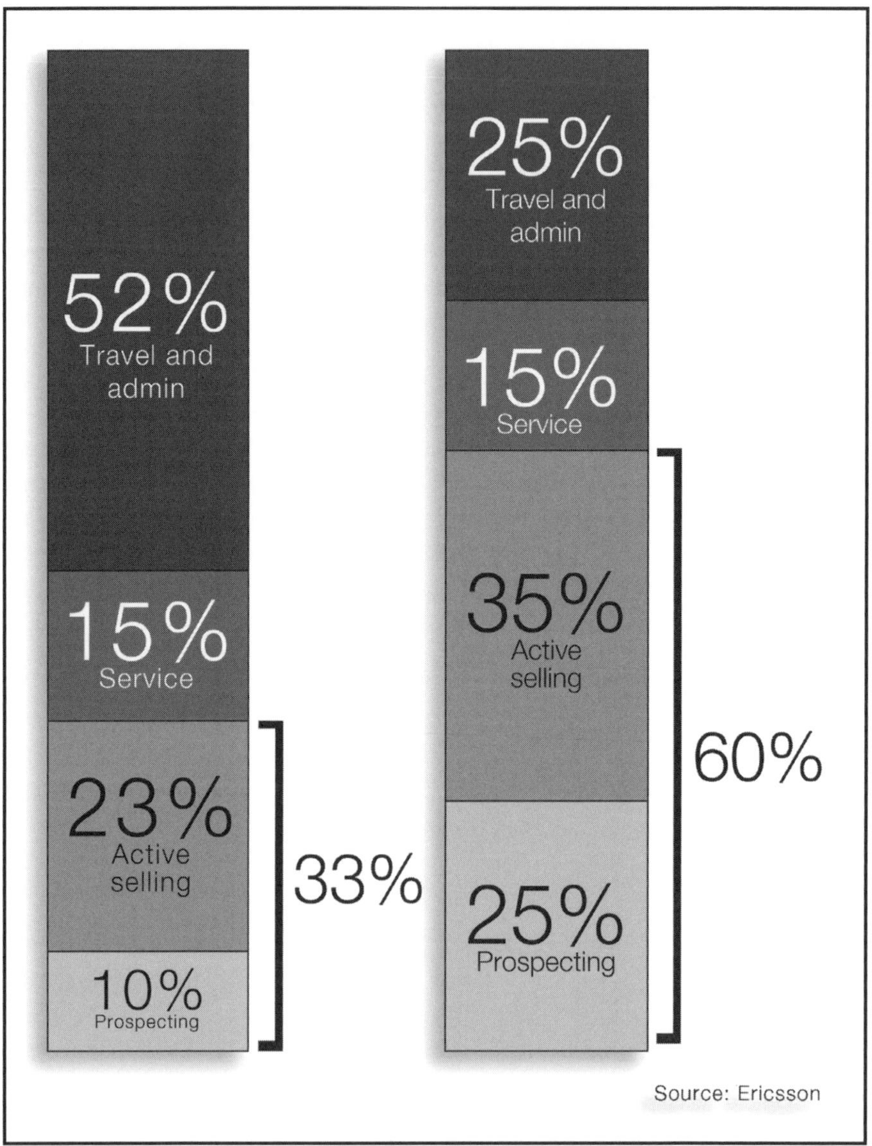
Salesperson's Time
52%
Travel and admin
15%
Service
23%
Active selling
10%
Prospecting
33%
25%
Travel and admin
15%
Service
35%
Active selling
25%
Prospecting
60%
Source: Ericsson

Freeing your sales team with technology and training

What is needed is the combination of technology and discipline. Remarkably, I still come across companies where managers say, 'We don't give our salespeople laptops or tablets, they might lose them', or, 'We haven't got a CRM (customer relationship management) system because it costs money.' Salespeople must first do their homework before visiting a prospective customer. You need to establish a probability of success (i.e. the lead turning into an order) for each prospect and salesperson should not be going out of the door unless there's a better than 50 per cent chance of getting the business.

You need a proper CRM system on which salespeople can report back. They don't need to be expensive but are only truly effective if there's a strongly-enforced discipline that *every* contact with the client or customer by anyone in the organisation (including you!) goes onto the system.

Next on the list is to ask if your salespeople – and by that I mean anyone who ever asks a customer for an order – have received any basic sales training? How can we expect these people to sell anything if they haven't been properly trained? How can we expect them to work their patch in an economical way unless they've been trained how to do so? I'd go even further and suggest that you would get big dividends if everyone in your organisation who ever talks to a customer for any reason – including credit control, for example – has training in basic sales skills.

Operational efficiency and the bottom line

It's not just about your salespeople and how they are spending their time. What about the rest of your people you have in your organisation? Are you and your managers really looking at how you maximise the time they spend doing what only they can do?

It's our job as business leaders, I suggest, to enable them to do their job and to make sure that they are doing the job only they can do. A former client of mine was a firm of land surveyors who weren't making any money. They had more than enough clients – and in that industry they charge by the hour. They kept recruiting more and more surveyors, but surprisingly nothing much happened to the bottom line.

I asked them what their bill/book ratio was – the hours billed to clients booked as a percentage of the total hours available – and they didn't know. So we worked it out for the previous year and it was below 30 per cent. No wonder the business wasn't making money!

What we found was that each surveyor really did what they wanted with no standardisation or paperwork and no thought about how they spent their, highly qualified, time. So we started with the senior surveyors and worked down through the organisation with the focus wholly on maximising the time they spent doing what only they could do. It took just over a year for the bill/book to move close to 70 per cent. Just imagine what that did to the bottom line! All we had to do was get them disciplined and make sure that we had the right people doing the right job.

If you have someone qualified to do something then that's what that person should spend the majority of their time doing. It may be common sense, but very few of us think like that.

Driving costs down

It's my experience that if you set your mind to reducing your overheads by 10 per cent you probably will. You just have to decide that you are going to – and it has to come from the top. It won't happen otherwise and it's easier to do than you think. You should assume that everything is negotiable. In the businesses I have run we had a policy that every service provider at least every three years went through a beauty parade – even our auditors. The accountants hated it, but every three years we got a massive reduction in our service bills. You can do the same, you just need to make up your mind to do it.

I have an engineering company client who recently won a contract worth £1.6 million. It just so happened that I was actually sitting in his office when he got the phone call from the customer saying they wanted to see him the next day to have the final discussions. I asked him if he would do something for me. Who would be the biggest supplier he would be placing orders with in order to complete the contract? He said it was a company in Yorkshire that makes electrical equipment so I asked him what those orders were likely to be worth. He said about £580,000.

I asked him to ring the managing director of that company right there and then and to use these words:

> I have just been told by a major new customer that we will be awarded an important contract tomorrow if we can sharpen our pencil. I'm prepared to commit to you that if I get the contract you will get the contract from me. What can you do on the price?

He was immediately given a 10 per cent reduction on the supplier's quote. That's £58,000 straight on to the bottom line.

After that we went through the next five suppliers and the average reduction he got was something like 6.8 per cent, just by asking.

You need to assume everything's negotiable. If you don't ask you don't get.

Dreaded discounting!

Now I have to talk about the two most dangerous words known to business: quantity discounting.

It always happens on a Friday morning, doesn't it? The sales manager knocks on your door and says, 'Boss, you know this big contract we've been after? All I need is a 10 per cent reduction and it's ours. But we need to sign now!'

Please, the next time that happens just stop and look at the mathematics.

Let's say you have a 30 per cent gross margin business. If you put your prices down by 10 per cent and you want the profit to stay exactly the same, how much more volume do you need to stand still? What do you think the maths says?

Twenty per cent?

No ...

It's 50 per cent!

But of course it isn't 50 per cent in reality. Because if you have 50 per cent more volume going through the business you'll probably have to pay overtime and perhaps you'll have to rent a warehouse or take on some other expense. It's probably nearer 60–70 per cent more volume you need – and all just to stay exactly where you were before you discounted.

Remember – the easiest thing to be in the game of business is a busy fool!

Pricing for your true value

Of course the other side of the coin is what happens if you put your prices up by 10 per cent? Again, keeping the profit exactly the same, how many customers can you afford to lose?

The maths here is 25 per cent. Maybe you can lose those bad payers and some of those difficult customers. I think that makes for a much healthier business.

I used to work for BTR which was one of the biggest corporations in the UK. If you were running one of their units, as I was, every year you were invited to London to meet with the CEO, Sir Owen Green, for a four-hour forensic examination of your budget.

I remember well that he would occasionally do a Colombo (the American TV detective) on me. I'd have my hand on the door on the point of leaving at the end of the four-hour meeting. A little smile would be appearing on his lips and he'd say, 'Just one thing ... What would happen if you put your prices up by 1 per cent at 9 o'clock tomorrow morning?'

Of course I would say, 'Not a lot I suppose really.' And he'd say, 'Well, we'll do that then shall we?'

That's a fair question for anyone in business and for you. What would happen if you put up your prices by 1 per cent tomorrow morning at 9 o'clock? Remember, there's something about price that doesn't apply to anything else. It goes straight on the bottom line to reinvest in the growth of your business.

In my experience, most of us undervalue ourselves, and particularly those of us running small businesses. It's time we stopped!

If you are having doubts, think about this. We know that supermarkets, for example, vary. In the UK we are likely to find cheaper prices in Asda, Lidl or Aldi. So why is it that Waitrose does so well? We know, as we walk in the door of Waitrose that we are going to pay more money for the same basket of shopping. So why do we do it? We go there because of the relationship and what's called 'customer intimacy' they have developed with us.

Those of us, like Asda or Lidl, who sell on price alone have to be driven by operational excellence and run our businesses with that driver preeminent.

Like Waitrose, however, most of us are in the business of 'perceived added value' and that means we need to be charging premium prices for whatever it is that we do and particularly for the relationship we have with our customers. The attitude you need to have throughout your entire organisation is one of being proud to be doing an outstanding job. You need to be thinking, 'We are giving outstanding value and we deserve higher prices.'

There's much more about all this in my book *Staying in the Helicopter®: The Key to Profitable Growth*.

Knowing your buyer's game

Every buyer in the world has a job to do. And that job is to try to turn your product or service into a commodity. Nirvana for them is that they buy your product or service at an internet auction. None of this relationship nonsense – that's their job, that's what they're paid to do!

In the days before the Iron Curtain fell I used to travel to countries where buyers would get badges for the 'scalps' (i.e. discounts) they got. If you walked into a room and saw lapels full of badges you knew you were going to be in for a hard time! It's still the same today.

You have to assume that any buyer is highly-trained and knows how to play the game of getting the best possible price.

Figure 11

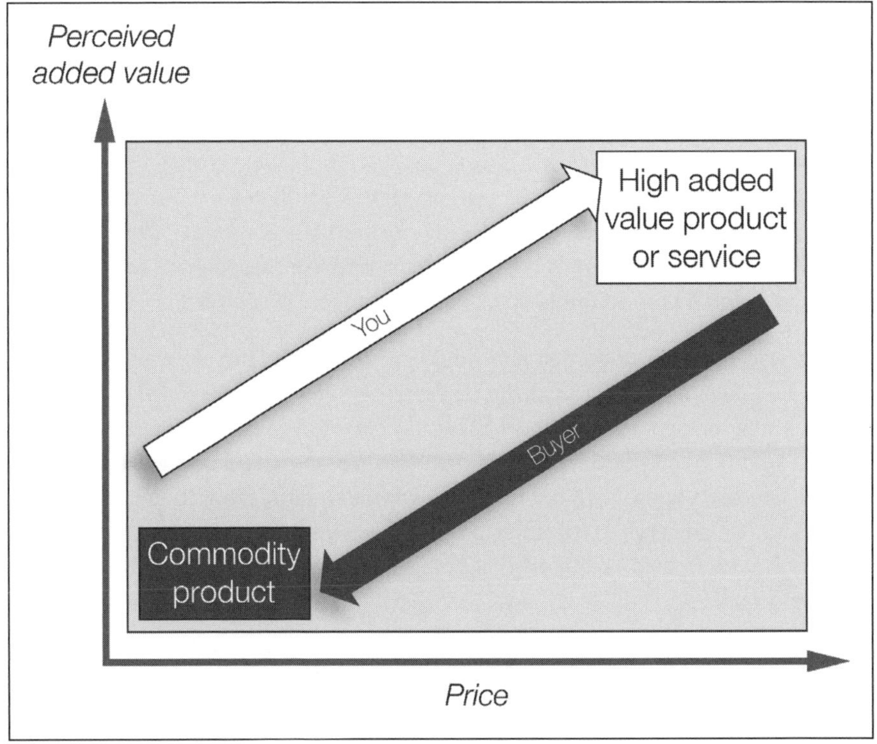

Never sell on price

Of course, it's your job and the job of your salespeople to do exactly the opposite; to turn the perception of whatever it is that you're selling into a higher value-added product or service.

In the list of reasons why customers buy your product, price *must* be below number three. I used to write this into my salespeople's contracts. They hated it. I've even had salespeople come to me and say categorically, 'We should have the lowest prices.' So I would say to them, 'I don't understand that. If we had the lowest prices we wouldn't need you!'

That reminds me, never give salespeople price discretion. They will give everything away. It's too easy. You are putting massive investment into this perceived added value of yours and it's their job to sell it. That's what they're there for.

It may be that in the recent harder economic times buyers think they have more power, so you have to know beforehand how you're going to respond if they play hardball. Please do not discount! If price is all about the value you give to your customer, then the moment you discount you are saying that your value is less. The psychology is wrong. If you really have to do something then give them 'stuff'. Give 'stuff' that costs you very little or nothing but that has a high perceived value to them.

Let me tell you about an experience I had. I received a phone call from a government owned organisation in the West Indies suggesting that I looked ideal to be the keynote speaker at their planned business excellence conference. 'You sound exactly right,' she said, which I took to be a fairly decent buying signal. I said, 'Fine', set my price and quoted a fee plus business class airfare and expenses. Then she rang back and asked if I would quote an all-inclusive price – which I did.

My wife and I then decided that she would join me on the trip, so we would go for four or five days and buy a package deal on the basis they were going to pay me for the whole thing, no matter how I spent the money. The client then came back to me and said they had never paid this much before and she didn't think she would get her director's approval. I did my homework and came back to her saying, 'I'm coming for five days now. I'm happy to come in early and do some media interviews if you'd like me to help fill the event. I noticed also that one of the sponsors of the event is a bank. As I'll be there anyway how about if I do a half-day workshop for them whilst I'm there – as part of the deal?'

She was delighted and came back to me within hours saying the bank was blown away by it and that they were going to fly in every branch manager from the whole of the Caribbean for the workshop. The contract came straight through and I got my fee without losing a penny. It didn't cost me anything, I just gave 'stuff' and all it cost me was a bit of my time. They even took my wife on a tour of the island while I was at the conference and we got to see leatherback turtles lay their eggs at two in the morning!

There's a lot most of us can give that actually costs us very little but has a high perceived value to our customers.

If finally you really do believe you have to give a discount please only do it in return for something that is not just the order. It might be some video testimonials, it might be a referral, but the psychology must be that our price is what it is because of the value we give. That's our price and we mean it.

We all buy irrationally, no matter what we're buying. It's all about perception, and we can change perceptions whether we are in retail or business-to-business the same applies.

Running business is about taking risks and the risks associated with increasing prices are small and, remember, you deserve higher prices!

59

Chapter Five
Back to
the Changing Rooms

Chapter Five Back to the Changing Rooms

So that's the four basics of business. If you were to do a health check on your business now how would you rate out of 100? What's acceptable, what score would let you sleep at night? Eighty-five? Ninety? Whatever it is, once again it's the dynamic that's important – that you are always moving forward.

Complete your scores now through the app and then check again in three months or six ... and the trend needs to be up if you are to continue winning in this new game of business. Maybe you could have each of your employees complete it – but please remember you must be prepared to both share the results and action them if you do.

Select the Four Basics of Business icon on the app Home screen

Figure 12

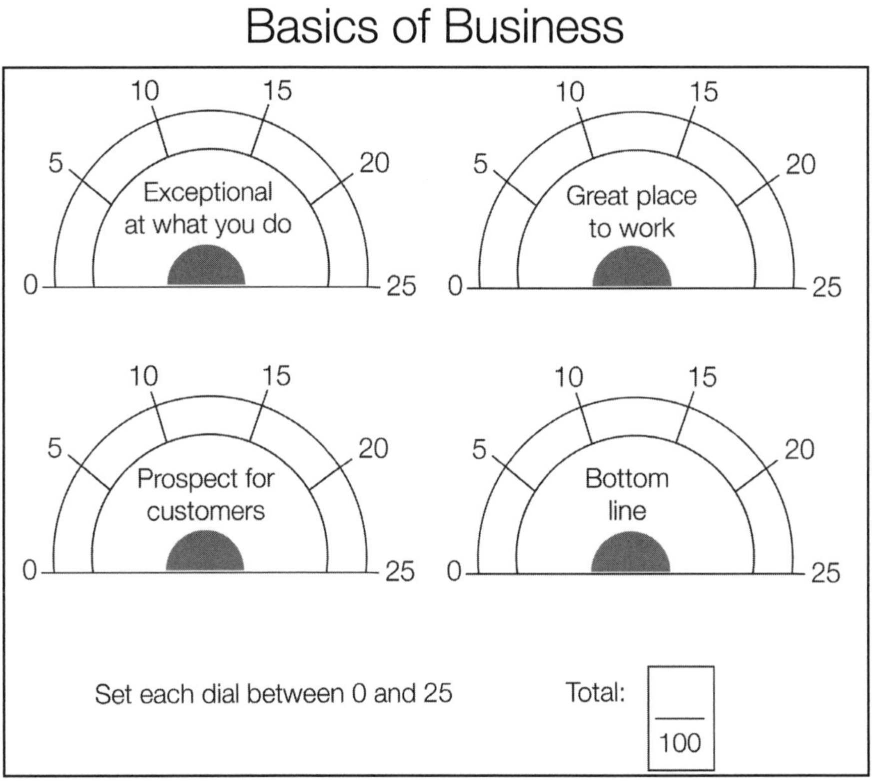
Basics of Business
Exceptional at what you do
Great place to work
Prospect for customers
Bottom line
0
5
10
15
20
25
Set each dial between 0 and 25
Total:
100

The Change House

What is clear is that if you are to win and keep winning, then change has got to be endemic in your organisation. There can be no paradigms that don't get challenged regularly. There needs to be a wall-to-wall culture of 'We can do better' and a massive reluctance to ever get complacent or arrogant.

Figure 13

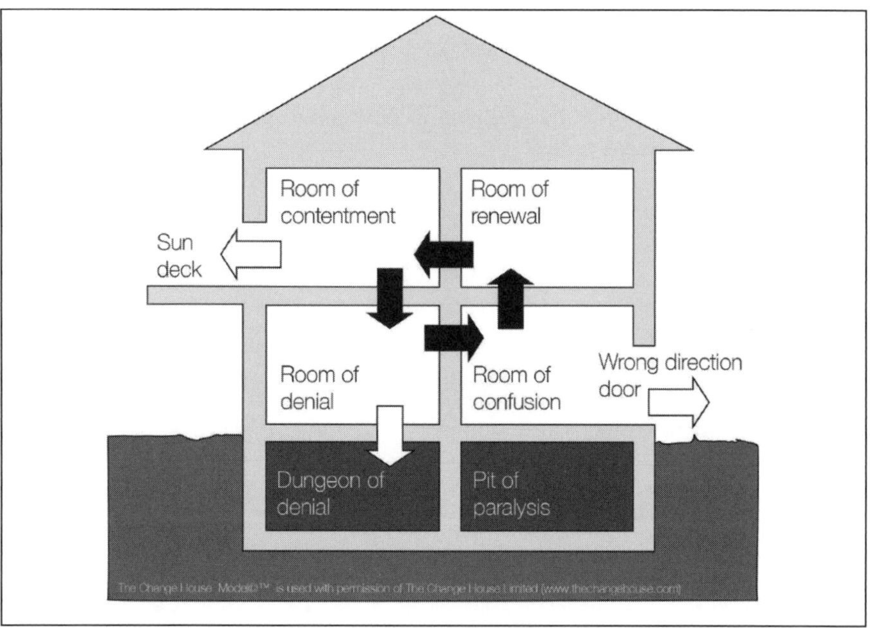

In the Change House model there are four rooms. Any individual, team or organisation, at any moment of time, is in one of these four rooms and can only move from room to room in a predetermined way.

In the room of contentment the culture is one of, 'We know exactly what we're doing. We have been the market leader for the last 10 years and our business model is the only business model. Go away!' That's where Coca-Cola was when Red Bull arrived. That's where Microsoft was when Search arrived and now Google are bigger than they are. That's where Caterpillar was when Komatsu arrived. That's where, in my experience, any government-owned organisation has great difficulty not being.

Ten years ago, Marks and Spencer in the UK were out on the sun deck. 'It's just so easy making money! We will never accept credit cards. We will never be at motorway service stations.'

Organisations in the room of contentment are characterised by a tendency towards smugness, complacency, arrogance and conceit.

Where do you go next from the room of contentment? There's no choice. It's the room of denial. This is where there's lots of finger pointing because it's all somebody else's fault. Always. It's the recession, it's the credit crunch, our market sector, the exchange rate, the government. It's the weather ... it's anyone but us. It's a bit like being an alcoholic, half the battle is recognising you are one. You need some sort of catalyst to get you out of the pit you're in. Otherwise, you end up down in the dungeon of denial. That's where the receivers are and you're still saying, 'Oh don't worry, it's just temporary; it's just a blip!'

That catalyst in a large organisation is often a new chief executive and usually a shaper (see Chapter One), someone who comes in and says, 'That's where we're going, follow me!' In a smaller organisation what you need is wholly objective, unsentimental advice and you won't get that from your family. You are most likely to get that from an outsider like an independent director, an adviser or colleagues in a peer group. You need somebody to say, 'Look, I think you're in denial and you need to do something about it!'

Assuming you *do* do something about it, your next destination is the room of confusion. This is where you're doing things half the old way and half the new way and it's all very confusing. There are revolving doors, new people coming, old people going and rumours are swirling around. One of the dangers is that employees might say to themselves, 'Look, for years we've been told we're going in this direction and now we're being told to go in this direction. Do you know the safest thing we can do? Keep our heads down.' Then they're in the paralysis pit and the whole place seizes up.

So leadership is at a real premium here. You have to keep repeating the message, 'This is where we're going, follow me.' There's also a danger of going through the wrong direction door, because it's all so confusing and so painful. You see a little bit of light and you say, 'That's got to be the way out,' and out you run and in reality it's not the right way.

Where you need to be trying to get to is the room of renewal. This is where you challenge every paradigm in your business. This is where absolutely nothing that you do is done simply because you have always done it that way. You pick everything up, look at it and you ask yourself if it's right for the future, yes or no? If it's 'no' then you throw it away. Even if it's the crown jewels that the business was built on, if it isn't right for the business tomorrow it has to go. The room of renewal is also where you're always raising the bar, and where you're always saying, 'But we can do better!'

There's a danger even when you're in the room of renewal because the room of contentment is very attractive and alluring. It's just there next door, trying to suck you over. I would argue that it may be difficult to get into the room of renewal but it's even harder to stay there. This is the only safe room to be in where your organisation is robust and prepared for almost any eventuality and where there are no signs of a resting on laurels or of complacency. Probably the single most important focus for any business, any organisation, is to work out not just how to get into the room of renewal but more importantly, how to stay there.

Select the Change House Animation icon on the app Home screen

So where are you and where's your organisation? To help you decide there's a short animation of the kinds of things I find people say in each of the rooms available through the app.

People tell me the Change House can be a great catalyst for discussion. Share it with your people and ask them the following:

- Where are you?
- Where's your department?
- Where's the business?

65

Chapter Six

The Final Level of the Game – Be a Winning Leader

Chapter Six The Final Level of the Game – Be a Winning Leader

If you are to be not just a winner but a serial winner as a leader in this new world of business then you need three things above all else and they are all heart things, not head things.

Belief, passion and courage

As a business leader, you've got to believe. You have to believe in whatever it is you're doing. If you don't believe, you'll get found out by your employees, by your financiers and your customers. If you don't truly believe in what you're doing don't do it!

You have to lead with a passion. Passion is not something you should leave at home, it should ooze out of the pores of your skin. Passion is infectious. People follow people with passion, it's what they need to see from you.

Finally you need courage. Businesses only move forward if you take risks. That's what your job is as a business leader – to take risks. Maybe we even have to take a few more risks than we used to. Whether it's the risk of setting the highest standards by your people, putting your prices up by a few per cent tomorrow, or the risk of trying out a new market – if you have the courage to focus mercilessly on the four basics of business in this book, I guarantee you will WIN!

I hope you enjoyed the book and found it useful in targeting your own business success. If so I'd love you to Tweet about it, comment on Amazon or LinkedIn – or in any other way you fancy!

Bibliography

Ericsson (2009) 'Aligning Operational Sales Efficiency towards New Customer Contact Strategies' talk given at Sales Excellence Forum, Warsaw, 16/17 March.

Philipson, A. (2014) 'Email is dead for today's students who prefer Twitter, universities say.' *The Telegraph*. [Online] Available at: http://www.telegraph.co.uk/technology/social-media/10864320/Email-is-dead-for-todays-students-who-prefer-Twitter-universities-say.html

Raffoni, M. (2010) 'Eight Things Your Employees Want From You.' *Harvard Business Review*. [Online] Available at: http://blogs.hbr.org/2010/03/important-reminders-for-anyone/

Roland Berger Strategy Consultants (2011) *Trend Compendium 2030*. Munich, Germany, p.112. [Online] Available at: http://www.rolandberger.com/gallery/trend-compendium/tc2030/

Also by Roger Harrop

Staying in the Helicopter®: The key to profitable growth

ISBN 978-0-9549586-1-9 (paperback)

ISBN 978-0-9567553-5-3 (kindle)

This is the must-have book for anyone running a business, or involved in running a business – from the smallest start-up to the largest corporate. Roger's twin themes of seeing the big picture by 'Staying in the Helicopter' and keeping it simple – because 'Business is simple it's only us that make it complex' – are applied to every aspect of business. He demonstrates his philosophy as he takes us through every aspect of business from business purpose, market leaders, profitable growth, finance, people, teams, hiring, leadership to change. Throughout we share Roger's real-life, down-to-earth experiences and simplified models from relevant international research. After reading this book you and your business will see significant benefit from the secrets and tools Roger has shared. Giving you sustained profitable growth – guaranteed!

Staying in the Helicopter®: The Key to Profitable Growth